MAKE A BETTER DEAL

A CONSUMER'S MANUAL

FOR NEGOTIATING WITH SALESPEOPLE

by

Matt Crawford

Table of Contents

Introduction

In this comprehensive guide, we will journey into the intricate world of sales and equip you with the knowledge and skills needed to effectively navigate the sales process. By understanding the psychology behind sales techniques, preparing thoroughly, and employing effective communication strategies, you can assert your needs, negotiate win-win solutions, and build strong relationships.

You may wonder why you should listen to me. I made a successful twelve-year career in the direct sales environment. I was a pushy door-to-door salesman, pushy car salesman, and a pushy in-home salesman. I worked for several companies, thinking that I would finally find the company who would put the customer first. That never happened, and I eventually came to a place where my conscience and sense of integrity would no longer allow me to encourage people to make poor decisions for the sake of a healthy paycheck. One of my past sales managers told me that customers have their own playbook and the sales manual was our playbook. I thought to myself that the customer does not have an adequate playbook. I hope that this book will help you to level the playing field and engage in future purchases from an offensive position that will ensure a better result for you, the customer.

Please keep in mind that, while some examples presented here do not necessarily apply to all salespeople or all companies, most of the information is common practice and widely taught. Companies expect their sales representatives to make use of specific tactics, but it is up to the individual salesperson to decide on their own level of ethical sales behavior.

Throughout this book, we will explore various topics such as the motivations and tactics of salespeople, developing strong relationships, recognizing and avoiding manipulative techniques, and negotiating ethically. We will also address the challenges posed by difficult salespeople and provide guidance on managing remote sales interactions. By the end of this book, you will have the tools to manage sales interactions with confidence, make informed decisions, and navigate the world of sales with ease. Let's embark on this journey together and unlock the art of negotiating with salespeople.

Chapter 1: Understanding the World of Salespeople

Defining Salespeople

Salespeople are professionals who are responsible for promoting and selling products, services, or ideas to customers. They play a crucial role in driving revenue for companies and bridging the gap between the organization and its customers. Salespeople can be found in any industry, including, but not limited to, retail, real estate, technology, healthcare, and more. Their primary objective is to persuade potential buyers to make a purchase or take a desired action.

Importance of Effective Communication with Salespeople

Effective communication with salespeople is essential for both buyers and sellers. It forms the foundation of successful sales interactions and ensures that the needs of both parties are met. By communicating effectively, buyers can convey their requirements, ask questions, and seek clarification; while salespeople can gather valuable information, address concerns, and tailor their offerings to meet the buyers' needs. Effective communication also fosters trust, transparency, and a mutually beneficial relationship between buyers and salespeople.

Common Misconceptions About Salespeople

1. Salespeople are pushy and manipulative: One of the most common misconceptions about salespeople is that they are overly aggressive and use manipulative tactics to persuade buyers. While it's true that some salespeople may resort to high-pressure techniques, it is important to recognize that not all sales professionals operate in this

manner. Most salespeople strive to build trust, understand customer needs, and provide valuable solutions.

2. Salespeople are only interested in making a sale: Many salespeople are solely focused on closing deals and maximizing their own profits. While salespeople have sales targets to meet, a skilled professional understands the importance of building long-term relationships and ensuring customer satisfaction. Successful salespeople prioritize meeting customer needs and creating mutually beneficial outcomes. It is important to note that many salespeople are working for a mutually beneficial outcome. However, there are a great number who rely solely on commissions for their livelihood. If they had to choose between providing for their families or cutting you a deal, they will always choose their families' needs first.

3. Salespeople have limited product knowledge: Some buyers assume that salespeople have a superficial understanding of the products or services they sell. However, a reputable salesperson invests time and effort in acquiring in-depth knowledge about their offerings. They are trained to provide accurate information, address customer concerns, and offer valuable insights to help buyers make informed decisions. Salespeople are always taught that product knowledge is key to their confidence about what they are selling. They are always continuing their education through mandatory or optional training, e.g. *In the car industry they often make their sales representatives obtain certifications before being able to sell specific products.*

4. Salespeople are not trustworthy: Trust is a critical component of any buyer-seller relationship. Unfortunately, salespeople sometimes face skepticism from buyers who believe they are not trustworthy or honest. While it is true that some individuals may engage in unethical practices, it is important to note this is not always the case. Many

salespeople strive to maintain their integrity, adhere to ethical standards, and prioritize the best interests of their customers. It is crucial to approach sales interactions with an open mind and avoid falling prey to the bias of stereotypes or misconceptions. By understanding the dynamics of sales interactions and building effective communication skills, buyers can navigate the world of salespeople with confidence and make informed decisions that align with their needs and goals.

Chapter 2: The Psychology of Salespeople

Salespeople operate in a dynamic and competitive environment. Understanding the psychology behind their motivations, tactics, and customer interactions can significantly enhance your ability to deal with them effectively. Salespeople are taught to believe in their products almost to the point of brainwashing. "I Am Sold Myself," or IASM, is drilled into the salesperson's thoughts. Whether it is true or not, they usually genuinely believe what they are telling you because a seasoned salesperson or company first sold them on the product and then promised them a six-figure income. This brainwashing begins on day one of their training and many salespeople do not know they are doing something wrong or unethical until they come to a realization of their own. At that point, they must decide if their conscience will allow them to continue with the company for the sake of a paycheck. We will explore the motivations and incentives that drive salespeople, the sales cycle they follow, the psychological tactics they employ, and the importance of building empathy and rapport.

Motivations and Incentives

Salespeople are often motivated by a combination of extrinsic and intrinsic factors. While financial rewards and commissions are common extrinsic motivators, intrinsic motivations such as personal fulfillment, recognition, and the desire to help others can also play a significant role. It is common practice for sales companies to have internal contests, not only for bragging rights and awards, but also for trips and other monetary prizes. Standard sales company practice is to hold sales representatives to a set of minimum metrics that are conducive to the company's bottom line. Sales metrics vary greatly by industry and include common themes such as "closing percentages," "client touchpoints," and a slew of other terms. Sales tactics could even be influenced by something as simple as wanting to avoid an uncomfortable conversation with their manager about why they couldn't close the sale. Many sales managers operate with the mentality that there is a sale in every interaction. Either the sales representative is selling you their product or service, or you are selling the sales representative on why you are not making a purchase. Understanding the motivations of salespeople can provide insights into their behavior, goals, and approach, enabling you to align your interactions with their needs and objectives.

Understanding the Sales Cycle

Salespeople typically follow a structured sales cycle that encompasses various stages from prospecting to closing a sale. Prospecting can be done in many ways such as knocking on your front door, emails, phone calls, advertising, sweepstakes, and many more. Prospecting is any action they take to get in front of a customer. Sales cycles are often separated into two categories. The short sales cycle, or a one call closing, convinces you to commit to a decision in the first interaction. The longer sales cycle will have multiple interactions before closing the deal. Stages may include identifying leads, conducting research, making initial contact, presenting solutions, handling objections, negotiating, and finally, closing the deal. Understanding the sales cycle allows you to anticipate the salesperson's actions, engage with them at the right time, and make informed decisions throughout the process.

Psychological Tactics Used by Salespeople

Salespeople employ a range of psychological tactics to influence buyer behavior and increase the likelihood of a sale. Some of these tactics would be:

1. Making a Friend: This is considered in many industries to be 70% of the sale. It is common knowledge that you are more likely to purchase from someone you like and trust. The difference between a good salesperson and a great salesperson is their ability to build rapport. The more successful you are in building rapport with the sales representatives, the more effective your objections become. Sales representatives have to walk a fine line between building comfort and rapport and creating a buddy situation that could give control of the sales process to you. By making a friend you can leverage their own sales tactics against them. This will be further discussed later in chapter five.

2. Reciprocity: Salespeople may offer something of value to the buyer. This can create a sense of obligation for you to reciprocate that kindness by making a purchase or engaging in conversation. Timeshare sales is a prime example of this tactic. You are offered a free or inexpensive vacation with the understanding that you will have to sit through an extensive sales presentation. Other examples of this tactic are complimentary lunches or even something as simple as a free gift.

3. Social Proof: By highlighting testimonials, case studies, or the popularity of a product or service, salespeople leverage social proof to influence buyer decisions. In this case, they will focus on positive information, but don't be fooled. Information can be easily twisted to reinforce desire or need for their product. Any good salesperson will be ready to counter the negative information you present. It is important to read and absorb the information presented to you and make informed decisions for yourself.

4. <u>Scarcity and Urgency:</u> Creating a perception of limited availability or time-sensitive offers can motivate buyers to act quickly and emotionally. The phrase, "this deal is only good for tonight" or "only for a limited time," is usually not the case. Sales managers will sometimes call you later to offer you an even better deal. In an ideal world, a sales representative will always provide you with the best possible deal before your interaction is concluded. Typically, however, there may be a second or third offer attempting to overcome your objections by providing additional value or reductions in price.

5. <u>Anchoring and Framing:</u> Salespeople use pricing strategies and presentation techniques to influence how buyers perceive the value and cost of a product or service. Their number one tactic when using pricing strategies is to convince you that the product pays for itself either immediately or over time through savings. They might walk you through a cost-benefit analysis or attempt to become your financial advisor. Be very wary of this tactic. Most companies only require a proven track record of success in sales for a representative to work for them, and the salesperson is not qualified to coach you on your finances. In some cases, it is true the product will save you more than it costs you to purchase it, but it is always important to understand all of the costs, fees, and variables involved. It is essential for you to do your own research, math, and due diligence in all sales interactions.

6. <u>Authority and Credibility:</u> Salespeople establish their expertise and credibility through knowledge, certifications, endorsements, and rapport. Often sales representatives are required to have regular continuing education in order to remain experts in their fields.

7. <u>One-of-a-Kind Products:</u> This is almost never the case. There is usually a similar product on the market that

is either equivalent to or better than what you are being shown - and often at a preferred price point.

8. Using Your Name: Everyone likes to hear their own name. Using your name regularly allows them to establish a sense of familiarity with you and promote rapport.

9. Emotion: Sales representatives are taught to use your emotions in a way that promotes making the sale. This is why most sales presentations take place in person. "When excitement is high, ask to buy," is a common saying in a sales training seminar. Presentations are designed to get you excited about a product so that you will make an emotional decision you normally wouldn't make. High emotional investment is another reason you may be asked to make a decision that day.

10. Your Children or Family: Many salespeople will use the well-being of your children or family against you. This is another way they can use your emotions to make a sale. By focusing on your family, they can maneuver you into a position that would create a situation where you would be likely to make an impulsive decision that you might not typically make. Think about how many mountains you would move to ensure your children or even your pets have the best quality of life you can afford. What wouldn't you do to make these special people's lives better? Seasoned sales representatives will hone in on this and hammer these pain points over and over again.

Recognizing these tactics can help you maintain objectivity, evaluate offers critically, and make decisions based on your needs.

Building Empathy and Rapport

Developing empathy and rapport with salespeople can foster a more collaborative and productive relationship.

By putting yourself in the salesperson's shoes, you can gain a deeper understanding of their challenges, goals, and pressures. Building rapport through active listening, showing genuine interest, and finding common ground creates a positive environment for effective communication and mutual respect. As mentioned before, "making a friend" can be used in your favor as well, allowing you an easy out with a salesperson if you are not interested in making a decision quite yet. Moreover, establishing rapport allows you to express your needs, concerns, and expectations more effectively, leading to a more tailored and satisfactory solution. Remember, empathy and rapport should not be confused with blindly accepting all sales propositions, but rather fostering a productive and respectful dialogue that benefits both parties. Keep in mind, sales representatives are also people and should be treated with respect, any negative interactions will hinder the overall sales interaction. It is always acceptable to politely end any interaction you no longer wish to continue.

By understanding the motivations and incentives of salespeople, the sales cycle they follow, the psychological tactics they employ, and the importance of building empathy and rapport, you will be better equipped to navigate sales interactions. In the next chapter, we will dive into the process of preparing for interactions with salespeople, enabling you to approach these interactions with confidence and clarity.

Chapter 3: Preparing for Interactions

To maximize the effectiveness of your interactions with salespeople, proper preparation is key. In this chapter, we will explore essential steps to take before engaging with salespeople, including setting clear objectives, conducting research on the salesperson and their company, analyzing your needs and requirements, and anticipating common sales techniques.

Analyzing Your Needs and Requirements

To effectively engage with salespeople, it is important to have a clear understanding of your own needs and requirements.

First, identify your "pain points." Pain points, or hot buttons, are the challenges or problems you wish to address with a product or a service, the benefits of a product or service, or simply the things you want, need, or are truly interested in having. Putting it simply, pain points are often the reason you seek the product or service in the first place. Understanding your pain points will enable you to communicate your needs more effectively to the salesperson. Pain points can become weaknesses that would lead you to making snap decisions you would not normally make. For example, if the product could benefit your family's health, your family's health could be your pain point. If you are in the market for a house and an attached garage is the most important aspect of the home you have in mind, the attached garage is your pain point. While you may need to indicate your desires or preferences during sales negotiations, be careful not to emphasize your pain points to a salesperson. The salesperson will be on the lookout for these and could potentially use them against you.

Next, prioritize features. Determine which features or aspects of the product or service seem most essential to you. This will allow you to focus on what really matters during the sales interaction and help you avoid getting overwhelmed and adding unnecessary things offered by the salesperson. It can be broken down into two categories - can I or can't I live without the feature. Remember, things you believe you cannot live without can quickly become pain points. However, it is important for you to be aware of your priorities before ever entering into a sales negotiation.

Last, but certainly not least, you must determine your budget. Establish a budget range or a maximum limit that aligns with your financial resources. This will help you evaluate pricing offers and negotiate within your boundaries. Staying within your budget will prevent you from having added financial stress and sales remorse. You may find you will have to edit some of your original priorities or preferences (and even some pain points) in order to stay within your budget. Staying within your budget should always be your number one priority.

Setting Clear Objectives

Before engaging with salespeople, it is crucial to define clear objectives for the interaction. What outcomes are you seeking? Are you looking to gather information, evaluate options, negotiate a deal, or simply learn more about a product or service? Clearly defining your objectives and sticking to them will guide your communication and ensure that you stay focused on what you want to achieve.

Conducting Research on the Salesperson and Their Company

Knowledge is power when dealing with salespeople. Conduct thorough research on the salesperson and their company to gain insights that can inform your interactions. Here are some aspects to consider:

1. <u>Company Background</u>: It is important to know and understand the history, size, and reputation of the salesperson's company. Research their industry position, reviews, values, and any recent news or developments that may be relevant. If you find yourself in an unexpected or surprise sales presentation, feel free to use your phone for an on-line search. The salesperson may ask you what you are doing, and you can very matter of factly say that you are researching the company. This act and reply will do two things. It will make them think you are interested, and it may throw them off their game by causing a bit of panic about what you might find.

2. <u>Product or Service:</u> Familiarize yourself with the features, benefits, and pricing of the product or service being offered. Compare it with alternatives available on the market to gain a better understanding of its value.

3. <u>Customer Reviews and Testimonials:</u> Seek feedback from other customers who have interacted with the salesperson or purchased similar products. One of the easiest ways to do this is through google reviews or any other online review source. Many salespeople are trained to obtain reviews before your interaction is concluded. These reviews can mention them by name, be about the company or the products and services they provide. This can provide valuable insights into the salesperson's credibility and the quality of their offerings. When reading reviews, always bring up the bad reviews first to keep the sales representative on their toes, but ultimately use your best judgment in determining how credible the reviews truly are.

Anticipating Common Sales Techniques

Salespeople often employ specific techniques to influence buyer behavior. By familiarizing yourself with these techniques, you can be better prepared to respond effectively. Some common sales techniques include.

1. Upselling and Cross-Selling: Salespeople may try to convince you to purchase additional products or services that complement your original choice.

2. Creating a Sense of Urgency: Salespeople may emphasize limited-time offers, discounts, or the risk of missing out on opportunities to encourage immediate action.

3. Overcoming Objections: Salespeople are trained to address any concerns or objections you may have and provide persuasive counterarguments. Sales teams hold weekly, if not daily, training dedicated to strategies for overcoming objections. The saying during the meeting is, "Isolate then overcome." All this means is, if they can isolate your objections down to one specific issue, it is easier for them to convince you to buy. You can handle this in one of two ways depending on your level of interest or readiness to move forward. If you are prepared to move forward, be upfront so you can get to a quick resolution. If you are not ready to move forward, be aloof and do not commit to one single objection no matter what they say to you.

4. Pricing Negotiations: Salespeople may employ various pricing strategies such as discounts, package deals, or value-added propositions. Some examples are advertising discounts, last year's model, friends and family discounts, urgency discounts, specials and many more. These discounts are quite often available every day. They are just using them to justify the price drop. *You are not a special case*! These discounts are available to everyone. By anticipating these techniques, you can maintain a clear understanding of your own needs and boundaries, critically

evaluate offers, and navigate the sales process more effectively.

By setting your objectives, conducting research, analyzing your needs, and anticipating common sales techniques, you can approach interactions with salespeople from a position of knowledge and confidence. In the next chapter, we will explore effective communication strategies that will help you navigate sales interactions with ease and assertiveness.

Chapter 4: Effective Communication Strategies

Effective communication is essential when dealing with salespeople. It enables you to convey your needs, gather information, handle objections, and negotiate with confidence. We will explore key communication strategies that will help you navigate sales interactions successfully - active listening, asking the right questions, managing objections, negotiations, assertiveness, and maintaining control.

Active Listening

Active listening is a fundamental communication skill that involves fully focusing on and comprehending the messages being conveyed. When interacting with salespeople, practice active listening by:

1. Paying Full Attention: Give the salesperson your undivided attention, maintain eye contact, and avoid distractions. This shows respect and allows you to fully understand their message. Learn and use their name just like they do yours. This helps make them feel familiar with you and believe you are invested in what they have to say.

2. Demonstrating Understanding: Use verbal and non-verbal cues, such as nodding or paraphrasing, to indicate that you are actively engaged and comprehending the information being shared.

3. Summarizing and Clarifying: Repeat or rephrase key points to ensure that you have accurately understood the salesperson's message. This helps avoid misunderstandings and demonstrates your attentiveness and desire for understanding. Get a notebook and pen and take notes. This not only helps you keep track of the presentation points, but it can put a small seed of doubt in

the mind of the salesperson that you aren't planning on making a decision today.

4. Avoiding interruptions: Allow the salesperson to complete their thoughts before responding. Again, you can take notes about what they are saying and the questions you may have. Any unanswered questions can be addressed when the salesperson asks for questions or at the end of the presentation. Interrupting can disrupt the flow of conversation and hinder effective communication. However, interruptions can be used to your advantage when they throw a salesperson off their game. Questions can have a similar result as conducting research on your phone in front of them. Another great tactic is to have someone with you. You can then ask the salesperson to step away so you have time to talk with each other. Do not hesitate to do this whenever necessary.

Asking the Right Questions

Asking the right questions is crucial for gathering information, clarifying details, and obtaining a deeper understanding of the product or service being offered. Consider the following question types when interacting with salespeople:

1. Open-Ended Questions: This type of question encourages the salesperson to provide detailed and informative responses rather than just yes or no answers. Examples include: "Can you tell me more about___," or, "How does this feature benefit me?" These more probing questions seek additional information or understanding about specific points. More examples would be, "Could you explain how this process works," or "Can you provide an example of how this has helped other customers?"

2. Clarifying Questions: These seek to ensure that you have correctly understood the information presented.

Examples include, "If I understand correctly, this product offers ___," or, "Could you clarify the warranty terms?"

3. Closing Questions: These help summarize the conversation and prompt the salesperson to address any remaining concerns or objections. Examples include, "Is there anything else I should know," or, "What are the next steps if I decide to proceed?" Asking relevant and thoughtful questions allows you to gather the information necessary to make informed decisions and demonstrate your engagement in the conversation. It also allows you to gauge the level of knowledge and trustworthiness of the sales representative. Some sales representatives will simply lie to you, make something up on the spot, or tell you what you want to hear. This is a dishonest sales representative. Honest sales representatives who cannot answer your question will say things like, "I don't know, but I know someone who will help me get you the right answer."

Managing Objections and Negotiation

In sales interactions, it is common to have objections and to want to negotiate terms. When negotiating with a sales representative they will usually only have one objection and it will be to you asking for a better price. Here are some strategies to effectively manage objections and engage in successful negotiation.

1. Stay Calm and Respectful: Approach objections or negotiation with a calm and composed demeanor. Avoid becoming defensive or aggressive, as this can hinder productive communication and desired result.

2. Seek Clarification: Ask follow-up questions to understand the basis of the salesperson's objection in order to negotiate from a place of mutual understanding. This demonstrates your willingness to address concerns and find common ground.

3. Present Alternatives or Solutions: Propose alternative options or solutions that can address the objections raised by the salesperson in order to meet both party's needs. This shows flexibility and a willingness to collaborate. You could say, "I'm not sure I need ___ or ___. Do you have another alternative that fits exactly what I'm looking for?"

4. Focus on Value: Emphasize the value or benefits of the product or service in relation to the objections raised. Help the salesperson understand how their offering aligns with your needs and objectives. It is acceptable to say things such as, "I only see the value of ___ in your product," or, "It only meets my needs in these ways ___."

5. Find Win-Win Outcomes: Approach negotiation with a mindset of seeking mutually beneficial outcomes. Strive for a solution that satisfies both your requirements and the salesperson's objectives. Be reasonable in your requests. It is unlikely the salesperson can give you 50% off of the product or services they are offering. While you might find their price ridiculous, they might feel the same about the price discount you request.

Assertiveness and Maintaining Control

Being assertive allows you to effectively communicate your needs, preferences, and boundaries while maintaining control of the conversation. This is very important because many salespeople are arrogant. I once had a fellow sales representative tell me he would ask for a cup of water with three ice cubes. He believed if someone gave him exactly what he asked for, he could do whatever he wanted in that customer's home and maintain control of the situation. While that belief may seem ridiculous, you must remember to stay in control. You must never let the salesperson believe he has all the control. Here are some tips for assertiveness.

1. Use "I Statements:" Express your thoughts and opinions using "I statements" to assert ownership of your perspective. "I statements" are often considered assertive because they convey personal thoughts, feelings, beliefs, or experiences in a direct and confident manner. They assert ownership and responsibility for one's own perspective or viewpoint without necessarily imposing it on others. For example, say, "I prefer ___," or "I need___"

2. Be Confident and Firm: Project confidence in your communication and maintain a firm but respectful stance. This helps ensure that your needs and objectives are taken seriously.

3. Set Boundaries: Clearly communicate your limits and boundaries, particularly regarding pricing, features, or any specific requirements. This helps establish the parameters for the discussion and avoids unnecessary pressure.

4. Take Time to Consider: Don't feel pressured to make an immediate decision. Take the time you need to reflect, gather additional information, or seek input from others before committing to an agreement. Even if you truly believe that the offer on the table is only good for today, be confident in the boundaries you set and walk away if necessary. That offer will probably still be available tomorrow.

By practicing active listening, asking the right questions, managing objections, negotiating effectively, and asserting yourself while maintaining control, you can navigate sales interactions with confidence, clarity, and mutual understanding. In the next chapter, we will examine the topic of building long-term relationships with salespeople and leveraging them to your advantage.

Chapter 5: Understanding Sales Tactics

Salespeople employ various tactics to influence buyer behavior and maximize sales. Understanding these tactics will enable you to navigate sales interactions more effectively. In this chapter, we will explore common sales tactics, including upselling and cross-selling, creating a sense of urgency, overcoming objections, and managing discounts and pricing negotiations.

Upselling and Cross-selling

Upselling is a tactic where salespeople encourage customers to purchase a higher-priced or upgraded version of a product or service. This is often done by focusing your interest on the cheaper product, then once you're interested, they show you something even better. For example, when you go to buy a specific used car, they let you test drive it, and then put you directly in a newer model. Once you have tasted something better, it is hard to go back to your original choice because now it feels inferior.

Cross-selling, on the other hand, involves suggesting additional products or services that complement the customer's original choice. You will be familiar with the basic example on Amazon. Once you put something in your cart, they list three or four different products that are usually purchased together. To manage the tactic of upselling and cross-selling:

1. Assess Your Needs: Determine your specific requirements and priorities before engaging with salespeople and then stick to those specifics. As mentioned earlier, identify your own pain points that you can and can't live without. Doing so will help you evaluate whether the

upsell or cross-sell aligns with your needs or is simply an attempt to increase the sale value for the salesperson.

2. Ask for Justification: If the salesperson proposes an upsell or cross-sell, inquire about the added value it provides. Understand how it enhances the original product or service and in order to determine whether or not it genuinely meets your needs.

3. Evaluate Cost-Effectiveness: Consider whether the upsell or cross-sell offers a reasonable return on your investment in terms of the additional cost. Assess whether the benefits outweigh the added expense.

Creating a Sense of Urgency

Creating a sense of urgency is a common tactic used to motivate buyers to make quick decisions. Salespeople may highlight limited-time offers, exclusive deals, or the risk of missing out. Here's how to approach this tactic:

1. Take Your Time: Don't succumb to pressure and rush into a decision. Evaluate the offer carefully and consider whether the sense of urgency is genuine or simply a sales tactic.

2. Request Additional Information: Ask for details about the time-sensitive offer or exclusive deal. Understand the actual deadline, the consequences of missing it, and whether or not the offer is truly beneficial for you. If you ultimately decide that it is in fact urgent and you feel like you have to go through with it, make sure you review and understand the cancellation policy. You should never feel any guilt about canceling after you do further research and decide it wasn't a good fit for you.

3. Consider Alternatives: Assess whether the sense of urgency is based on the uniqueness of the offer or if comparable options exist in the market. Evaluate whether there are alternative products or services that can meet your

needs without the time pressure. There will almost always be another option. If someone truly had a one-of-a-kind unique product or deal why would they need to make it time sensitive?

Overcoming Objections

Salespeople are trained to address objections and concerns that potential buyers may have. Some common objections they are trained to deal with are the spousal objection that could be raised by your significant other if that partner isn't present, hearing you say, "I need to think about it," or "Not today," sticker shock, and many more. To handle objections effectively:

1. Listen Actively: Allow the salesperson to fully express their response to your objection. Pay attention to their reasoning and evaluate if it addresses your concerns adequately. You should become immediately concerned if the sales representative answers your question evasively or redirects you back to their point. For instance, if you ask a simple question about something, such as the overall price or interest rate, and you are given a well-crafted and practiced line followed up with redirecting your focus to the payment without answering your original question, consider this is an automatic red flag and follow the next steps.

2. Seek Clarification: If the salesperson's response is unclear or does not fully address your objection, seek further clarification. Ask for additional information or examples that illustrate their point.

3. Trust Your Instincts: If the salesperson's response does not alleviate your concerns or, if you still have doubts, trust your instincts. Don't be afraid to express your continued reservations or seek alternative solutions.

Handling Discounts and Pricing Negotiations

Salespeople often use discounts and pricing negotiations to close deals. Sales representatives practice giving these discounts or price drops countless times with their peers. They will often go as far as to call a manager over to speak with you or, if in your home, make a phone call to the manager. These managers usually have many years of sales experience and there is a reason why they are in their position. They are not in these positions due to their ability to manage individuals, it's usually their ability and track record in closing sales. You should be more guarded and cautious with them than you are with the original sales representative. To navigate these situations.

1. Understand the Value: Evaluate whether the discounted price aligns with the value you perceive in the product or service. Consider factors such as quality, features, and long-term benefits when determining if the price is reasonable.

2. Research Alternatives: Compare the offered price with similar products or services available in the market. This will help you gauge the competitiveness of the offer and negotiate from an informed position. If anyone ever tells you this is the only product on the market that does what it does, immediately do your research.

3. Negotiate with Confidence: If you believe the price is negotiable or, if you have identified specific terms that need adjustment, enter into negotiations confidently. Clearly articulate your reasons for requesting a different price and be prepared to justify your position. I do not recommend accepting the first offer, nor will the sales representative expect that you will. They are trained to skillfully make price drops until they get to their bottom dollar. Bottom dollar is a term used in the sales world that just means the price at which the company and sales representative will no longer make a profit or commission worth the company's time. Remember you have the power.

The sales representative generally wants your money more than you want their product. You have the money; you have the power.

4. <u>Consider the Overall Package:</u> Instead of solely focusing on the price, assess the overall value proposition, including warranties, customer support, or additional benefits. Evaluate the entirety of what is being offered before finalizing your decision.

5. <u>Always ask these Mandatory Questions:</u>

- Are there any additional costs?
- What kind of warranty does it come with?
- What does it cost to maintain?
- Be very specific and make sure you understand what is involved and the terms of your warranty.
- If your purchase involves a loan, ask the following questions:
- What is the overall price?
- What is the interest rate?
- What is the term of the loan?
- What kind of loan is this?
- Are there any hidden fees I should know about?
- What is the cancelation policy?

Even if you believe the salesperson has given you a straight and honest answer, always read your entire contract. These might seem like common sense questions but many sales people operate under a don't ask, don't tell policy. You would be surprised how many people will get excited and just sign on the dotted line just because they can afford a monthly payment.

By understanding sales tactics such as upselling and cross-selling, creating a sense of urgency, overcoming objections, and handling discounts and pricing negotiations, you can navigate sales interactions more effectively and make informed decisions. In the next chapter, we will discuss building long-term relationships with salespeople and leveraging them to your advantage.

Chapter 6: Building Strong Relationships

Building strong relationships with salespeople can bring numerous benefits, such as gaining access to valuable insights, receiving personalized assistance, and obtaining favorable terms. We will explore key strategies for building long-term relationships with salespeople, including establishing trust and credibility, fostering partnerships, utilizing effective communication channels, and finding the balance between assertiveness and cooperation.

Trust and Credibility

Trust and credibility are the foundation of any successful relationship. When dealing with salespeople, establishing trust is crucial. Here are some ways to build trust:

1.<u>Consistency:</u> Be consistent in your interactions and follow through on your commitments. This shows reliability and integrity, which are essential for establishing trust.

2. <u>Honesty and Transparency:</u> Communicate openly and honestly with salespeople. Clearly express your needs, expectations, and any concerns you may have. This promotes trust and fosters a more productive relationship.

3. <u>Deliver on Your Promises:</u> If you agree to certain terms or commitments, ensure that you follow through on them. Meeting your obligations demonstrates your reliability and reinforces trust. If at any point you find your sales representative has lied to you or misled you in any way, this is a breach of your trust. Do not feel obligated to continue with them and always be comfortable canceling the transaction.

Developing Long-Term Partnerships

Long-term partnerships with salespeople can be mutually beneficial. Consider these strategies to develop and nurture such partnerships.

1. <u>Shared Goals and Values:</u> Seek salespeople who align with your goals and values. Look for individuals or companies that prioritize customer satisfaction and long-term relationships over short-term gains. For example, if a company sells you a product and expects you to take immediate ownership of it, such as installing a product the next day, this is not typically for your benefit. Instant installation is a widely used tactic for in-home sales representatives. It makes it harder for you to think about your decision or back out. Salespeople will make you feel that installing quickly is a plus to buying from them, but if it helps ensure a sale it is mostly for their benefit not yours. If this is convenient for you and you are prepared for immediate possession, feel free to agree, but be sure you take ownership of your purchase on your own terms.

2. <u>Provide Feedback:</u> Offer constructive feedback to salespeople based on your experiences. This helps them understand your preferences and expectations, allowing them to better tailor their offerings to your needs. Do not hesitate to write truthful reviews whether good or bad.

3. <u>Seek Their Expertise:</u> Salespeople have extensive knowledge about their products or services. Tap into their expertise by seeking advice or insights on industry trends, emerging technologies, or potential solutions to your challenges.

4. <u>Referrals:</u> If you are happy with and trust your sales representative and their company, do not hesitate to give them referrals. Make sure the people you refer fully understand the sales process and cycle you went through

before they interact with the sales representative. They will appreciate being prepared beforehand.

Effective Communication Channels

Choosing the right communication channels is vital for maintaining strong relationships with salespeople. Consider the following:

1. <u>Face-to-Face Meetings:</u> Whenever possible, opt for face-to-face meetings, either in person or via video conference. This allows for more personal and meaningful interactions, fostering stronger relationships. Sales representatives often prefer this because it's easier to get a resolution this way. It will make the process easier for you too.

2. <u>Phone or Email Communication:</u> Use phone calls or emails for routine or non-urgent matters. This provides a convenient way to stay in touch and address any queries or concerns. If a sales representative is non-responsive after the sale, do not hesitate to call their company and hold them accountable for any and all promises.

3. <u>Online Platforms and Communities:</u> Engage with salespeople through online platforms and communities specific to their industry or product. This can facilitate networking, knowledge sharing, and continuous learning.

Positive and respectful communication skills are vital in maintaining relationships and negotiating deals that benefit you.

Balancing Assertiveness and Cooperation

Maintaining a healthy balance between assertiveness and cooperation is crucial when dealing with salespeople. You never want to seem aggressive or confrontational.

1. <u>Be Clear:</u> Clearly communicate your needs, expectations, and boundaries from the beginning. This sets the foundation for a productive relationship and avoids misunderstandings.

2. <u>Advocate for Yourself:</u> Be assertive in expressing your preferences and objectives. Articulate your requirements and negotiate when necessary. Remember that a balanced approach allows you to advocate for your needs while still fostering cooperation.

3. <u>Listen and Be Open to Suggestions:</u> Salespeople may have valuable insights or alternative solutions that can benefit you. Remember they often have key insights and extensive product knowledge. Motivated sales representatives might even offer you a cheaper solution that can meet your needs. Be open to their suggestions and actively listen to their recommendations. Cooperative attitudes foster collaboration and strengthen relationships.

4. <u>Seek Win-Win Outcomes:</u> Strive for win-win outcomes where both parties feel satisfied with the results. Look for mutually beneficial solutions that address your needs while considering the salesperson's goals and limitations. They often work for commission and have to protect the company's bottom dollar. Your wishes may be unreasonable. Any reputable company may not be able to accommodate your wishes when what you desire is not legal or up to code. You never want to work with a company who cuts corners.

By establishing trust and credibility, developing long-term partnerships, utilizing effective communication channels, and finding the balance between assertiveness and cooperation, you can build strong relationships with salespeople. These relationships can enhance your buying experience, provide valuable support, and lead to better outcomes. In the next chapter, we will explore strategies for handling difficult or unethical sales practices.

Chapter 7: Recognizing and Avoiding Manipulative Techniques

During sales interactions, it's important to be aware of manipulative techniques that certain salespeople may employ to influence your decision-making. By recognizing and avoiding these tactics, you can protect yourself from unethical practices and make informed choices. We will continue by learning how to recognize high-pressure tactics, spot deceptive sales practices, trust your instincts, and effectively set boundaries and assert your needs.

Recognizing High-Pressure Tactics

High-pressure tactics are designed to push you into making a quick decision without fully considering your needs or alternatives. Here are some signs of high-pressure tactics:

1. Urgency and Scarcity: Salespeople may create a false sense of urgency by emphasizing limited-time offers, exclusive deals, or claiming that the product or service will no longer be available tomorrow.

2. Aggressive or Pushy Behavior: Salespeople who employ high-pressure tactics may use aggressive or forceful language, constantly interrupt you, or disregard your objections and concerns.

3. Manipulative Emotional Appeals: They might try to manipulate your emotions by playing on fear, guilt, or the desire for social approval, making it harder for you to think objectively.

4. Excessive Flattery or Compliments: Salespeople may use flattery or excessive compliments to win your favor while making you feel obliged or indebted to them,

creating an environment that makes it more difficult for you to decline their offer.

Recognizing these tactics will alert you to take a step back, proceed with caution, evaluate the situation objectively, and carefully consider the deal in order to make decisions that align with your best interests.

Spotting Deceptive Sales Practices

Deceptive sales practices involve misleading or false information that aim to manipulate your perception or decision-making. These tactics are utilized most often during what is called the closing process, the time after they have asked for your order. Here are some warning signs of deceptive sales practices.

1. Misrepresentation of Facts: Salespeople may misrepresent the features, benefits, or limitations of a product or service to make it appear more appealing or suitable to your needs. Touting their product as unique to the market and nothing else will do what it does is a very common misrepresentation of the facts. It may even be a blatant lie.

2. Hidden Costs or Conditions: Salespeople may omit or downplay additional costs, fees, or contractual obligations that may impact the overall value or long-term commitment required. If something involves a loan, make sure you fully understand the terms of that loan and the sales cancelation policy before signing.

3. Pressure to Make Immediate Decisions: Deceptive salespeople may try to prevent you from seeking alternative opinions or conducting thorough research by insisting on an immediate decision. Be prepared to walk away from the sale.

4. Lack of Transparency or Clarity: If a salesperson avoids providing straightforward answers to your questions

or evades specific details, it is almost always a red flag indicating deceptive practices.

Being aware of these deceptive tactics allows you to ask probing questions, verify information independently, and make well-informed decisions.

Trusting Your Instincts

Trusting your instincts is an essential skill when dealing with salespeople. If something feels off or too good to be true, it's important to listen to your gut feeling. Here's how to build confidence in your instincts:

1. Take Your Time: Allow yourself time to reflect on the situation. Don't rush into decisions if you have doubts or concerns. Trusting your instincts often means taking a step back and evaluating the situation more carefully.

2. Gather Information: Conduct thorough research, seek recommendations from trusted sources, or read reviews to gain a broader perspective. This helps validate your instincts and provide additional information for decision-making.

3. Consider past experiences: Reflect on past interactions or experiences with salespeople. If you've had negative encounters or felt manipulated before, use those experiences as a reference point to inform your judgment.

4. Seek a Second Opinion: If you're unsure about a salesperson's claims or tactics, consult a trusted friend, family member, or professional who can provide an objective viewpoint. They may offer insights that can help you make a more informed decision.

Trusting your instincts empowers you to make decisions that align with your values and protect your best interests.

Setting Boundaries and Asserting Your Needs

Setting boundaries and asserting your needs are crucial to sales interactions that lead to positive results for you. Here's how to effectively establish and communicate your boundaries:

1. Define Your Requirements Ahead of the Sales Meeting: Clearly identify your needs, preferences, and limitations before engaging with salespeople. This gives you a clear reference point when communicating your boundaries.

2. Communicate Assertively: Clearly express your boundaries and expectations to the salesperson. Use assertive communication techniques to convey your needs while remaining respectful and firm. Remember your "I statements."

3. Be Prepared to Walk Away: If a salesperson consistently disregards or violates your boundaries, be prepared to walk away from the transaction. It's essential to prioritize your well-being and not engage with individuals who do not respect your boundaries.

4. Seek Alternatives: If a salesperson is unable or unwilling to meet your needs or respect your boundaries, explore alternative options. There are often multiple providers or solutions available, and finding one that aligns with your requirements is crucial.

Setting boundaries and asserting your needs ensures that you maintain control over the buying process and that transaction outcomes are in your best interest. By recognizing high-pressure tactics, spotting deceptive sales practices, trusting your instincts, and effectively setting boundaries and asserting your needs, you can navigate sales interactions with confidence and protect yourself from manipulation. In the final chapter, we will provide a summary of key takeaways and offer additional resources for further support.

Chapter 8: Negotiating Win-Win Solutions

Negotiation is an essential skill when dealing with salespeople. It allows you to find mutually beneficial outcomes and achieve the best possible results. In this chapter, we will explore the principles of effective negotiation, identifying common ground, creating mutually beneficial outcomes, and understanding when to walk away from a negotiation.

Principles of Effective Negotiation

To negotiate effectively with salespeople, keep these principles in mind.

1. Preparation: Whenever possible, do your research and gather information about the product, market value, and competitive offerings. Understand your needs, priorities, and desired outcomes before entering into negotiations.

2. Active Listening: Listen carefully to the salesperson's perspective and understand their interests and concerns. Actively listening allows you to identify areas of potential agreement and find common ground.

3. Flexibility and Creativity: Approach negotiations with an open mind. Be willing to explore creative solutions that meet both your needs and the salesperson's objectives.

4. Win-win Mindset: Adopt a win-win mindset, seeking outcomes that satisfy both party's interests. Look for solutions where both you and the salesperson feel like you have gained value from the negotiation.

5. Focus on Interests, not Positions: Instead of getting fixated on specific positions or demands, focus on underlying interests. Understanding the salesperson's

motivation will help you identify alternative solutions that can satisfy both parties.

Identifying Common Ground

Finding common ground is essential for successful negotiation. Here's how to identify areas of agreement.

1. Shared Objectives: Identify shared objectives or goals that both you and the salesperson want to achieve. Emphasize these shared interests to build rapport and foster collaboration.

2. Needs and Priorities: Understand the salesperson's needs and priorities. Look for areas where your requirements align, allowing you to work together towards a mutually beneficial outcome.

3. Problem-Solving Approach: Adopt a problem-solving mindset rather than an adversarial one. Focus on finding solutions that address both your needs and the salesperson's challenges.

4. Open Communication: Encourage open and honest communication to ensure that both parties have a clear understanding of each other's perspectives and concerns. This promotes a cooperative environment for negotiation.

Creating Mutually Beneficial Outcomes

Negotiations should aim for outcomes that benefit both you and the salesperson. Why should a sales representative want to work with you when you are unwilling to work with them? Consider these strategies to create mutually beneficial solutions:

1. Explore Trade-Offs and Compromise: Identify areas where you can make concessions that are of lower importance to you but hold value for the salesperson.

Similarly, seek concessions from the salesperson that fulfill your priorities.

2. Keep Your Options Open: Look for opportunities to expand the value or benefits of the negotiation. Find ways to create additional value that can be shared by both parties, such as exploring additional services, extended warranties, or partnership opportunities. Research the other options and pick the best additional services for your lifestyle.

3. Build Long-Term Relationships: Consider the potential for building a long-term relationship with the salesperson or their company. Taking a collaborative approach and nurturing a positive relationship can lead to future opportunities and added benefits. Certain large expense purchases, such as cars or in-home installations, may require a long-term relationship with the company.

4. Seek Creative Solutions: Think outside the box and explore alternative options that satisfy both party's interests. Brainstorming creative solutions can lead to innovative win-win outcomes.

Knowing When to Walk Away

Sometimes, despite your best efforts, a mutually satisfactory agreement may not be possible. It's important to recognize when to walk away from a negotiation.

1. Unreasonable or Non-Transparent Pricing: If you believe the price being offered is unfair or if the seller is not providing clear and transparent information about pricing components, it may be wise to walk away and explore other options.

2. High-Pressure Tactics: If the salesperson is using aggressive or manipulative tactics to coerce you into making a purchase, it's generally a red flag. Walking away

from such a situation can help protect your interests and prevent any potential regrets.

3. Misleading or False Information: If you discover that the seller is providing misleading or false information about the product or service, it's a sign of dishonesty. Walking away is a reasonable response to protect yourself from making a purchase based on inaccurate information.

4. Lack of Trust or Integrity: If you have reason to doubt the trustworthiness or integrity of the seller or the company, it's essential to prioritize your own peace of mind. Walking away from the negotiation can help you avoid potential issues or regrets.

5. Unsatisfactory Terms or Conditions: If the terms and conditions of the sale are unacceptable or do not align with your needs, it will be better to walk away and explore other options that offer more favorable terms.

6. Poor Customer Service or Lack of Responsiveness: If the salesperson or the company consistently displays poor customer service, doesn't address your concerns, or fails to respond to inquiries in a timely manner, it may be an indication of potential future issues. Consider walking away and finding a business that values your satisfaction.

Knowing when to walk away is an essential skill to develop that makes you able to protect yourself and ensure that you don't agree to terms or conditions that are not in your best interest. If you are not happy with your sales representative and really want to pursue purchasing the product, feel free to request a different representative. If they do not wish to accommodate you, feel free to move on. By following the principles of effective negotiation, identifying common ground, creating mutually beneficial outcomes, and understanding when to walk away, you can navigate negotiations with salespeople more confidently and achieve win-win solutions. In the final chapter, we will recap the key points discussed throughout the book.

Chapter 9: Ethical Considerations

Ethics play a crucial role in sales interactions. Maintaining ethical standards ensures fairness, trust, and long-term relationships. In this chapter, we will discuss the importance of transparency and honesty, ethical decision-making in sales interactions, recognizing unethical practices, and setting ethical standards for yourself.

Transparency and Honesty

Transparency and honesty are fundamental pillars of ethical conduct in sales. Here's why they matter:

1. Building Trust: Being transparent and honest builds trust between you and the salesperson. Trust is essential for fostering a positive and mutually beneficial relationship.

2. Long-Term Relationships: Transparency and honesty contribute to building long-term relationships based on integrity and reliability. This can lead to continued collaboration and enhanced customer satisfaction.

3. Reputation and Credibility: Conducting yourself with transparency and honesty safeguards your reputation and credibility. People are more likely to engage in business with those who are known for ethical behavior.

Ethical Decision-Making in Sales Interactions

Making ethical decisions in sales interactions is crucial for maintaining integrity. Consider these factors when making ethical decisions:

1. Balancing Interests: Consider the interests of all parties involved, including your own, the salesperson's, and any other stakeholders such as family members. Strive for outcomes that are fair and respectful to all parties.

2. <u>Compliance with Laws and Regulations:</u> Ensure that your actions align with relevant laws, regulations, and industry standards. Adhering to legal requirements sets the foundation for ethical conduct.

3. <u>Consistency with Values:</u> Align your decisions with your personal or organizational values. Make choices that reflect your principles and contribute to a positive ethical climate.

4. <u>Realizing Long-term Consequences:</u> Evaluate the potential long-term consequences of your decisions. Ethical decision-making involves looking beyond immediate gains and considering the impact on relationships, reputation, and sustainability.

Recognizing Unethical Practices

Recognizing unethical practices is essential to protect yourself and make informed decisions. Here are some signs of unethical sales practices:

1. <u>Misleading or False Information:</u> Salespeople may provide inaccurate or misleading information to manipulate your decision-making process. Some may rely on half-truths, while others may openly lie. The more you prepare prior to the meeting, the more likely it is that you will recognize inaccurate information.

2. <u>High-Pressure Tactics:</u> Salespeople using coercive or manipulative techniques to push you into deciding against your better judgment. Be aware of your emotional triggers and desire for the product so you will be more aware of this type of manipulation.

3. <u>Hidden Fees or Conditions:</u> Salespeople intentionally omitting or downplaying important fees, contractual obligations, or limitations associated with a product or service are not acting in your best interest. Read

the fine print and understand all documents before committing to a purchase.

4. Lack of Transparency: Salespeople avoiding or deflecting questions, or being evasive when providing information, can be indicative of unethical practices. If a salesperson is unwilling to answer your questions or glosses over information, be prepared to move on to another opportunity.

5. Unprofessional Behavior: Salespeople displaying unprofessional conduct, such as disrespect, aggression, or engaging in unethical sales strategies, should raise ethical concerns. If a salesperson acts in a disrespectful manner, firmly, yet respectfully and unemotionally, cut off negotiations and seek to make your purchase elsewhere or with another company salesperson.

Being vigilant and observant allows you to identify unethical practices and take appropriate action.

Setting Ethical Standards for Yourself

Setting ethical standards for yourself establishes a framework for your behavior in sales interactions. Consider these steps:

1. Define Your Values: Clarify your personal or organizational values and principles. Know what you believe and what you stand for when entering into a sales negotiation. This forms the basis for your ethical standards and guides your decision-making.

2. Educate Yourself: When uncertain about forming ethical guidelines, become informed about ethical transactions and best practices. Continuously educate yourself to ensure your actions align with current ethical standards.

3. Reflect on Dilemmas: Reflect on ethical dilemmas you encounter and consider the best course of action. Engage in ethical discussions and seek guidance from mentors or trusted advisors when facing challenging situations.

4. Seek Accountability: Hold yourself accountable for upholding ethical standards. Be open to feedback and learn from your experiences to continually improve your ethical decision-making.

Setting ethical standards for yourself reinforces your commitment to integrity and ensures that your actions align with your values and principles. You should not expect more from the salesperson than you do from yourself. If you expect your sales representative or their company to be ethical, you should be as well. Respectful interactions are a two-way street. By prioritizing transparency and honesty, practicing ethical decision-making, recognizing unethical practices, and setting ethical standards for yourself, you can navigate sales interactions with integrity.

Chapter 10: Dealing with Difficult Salespeople

Interacting with difficult salespeople can be challenging, but it's important to maintain professionalism and handle such situations effectively. We will discuss how to identify challenging personality types, handle aggressive and pushy salespeople, resolve conflicts professionally, and employ assertive communication strategies.

Identifying Challenging Personality Types

Understanding different personality types can help you navigate difficult sales interactions more effectively. Here are some common challenging personality types you may encounter:

1. Aggressive and Pushy: These individuals use forceful tactics, apply high-pressure sales techniques, and may disregard your objections or concerns.

2. Manipulative and Deceptive: Salespeople with manipulative tendencies may use misleading information or false promises to influence your decision-making.

3. Evasive: Sales representatives who will never give you a straight answer and try to avoid directly answering your questions or addressing your needs and concerns.

4. Passive-Aggressive: These individuals may appear cooperative on the surface but subtly undermine your interests or use passive-aggressive behavior to manipulate you and gain an advantage.

5. Overly Demanding: Salespeople who exhibit overly demanding behavior may have unrealistic expectations or put excessive pressure on you to meet their demands.

Recognizing these personality types allows you to prepare and respond appropriately during interactions.

Handling Aggressive and Pushy Salespeople

Dealing with aggressive and pushy salespeople requires tact and assertiveness. Here's how to handle such situations effectively.

1. <u>Stay Calm and Composed:</u> Maintain your composure and avoid reacting impulsively to their aggressive behavior. Take deep breaths and focus on staying centered and collected.

2. <u>Set Firm Boundaries:</u> Clearly communicate your boundaries and expectations. Assertively express your needs and priorities, making it clear that you won't be swayed by aggressive tactics.

3. <u>Be Assertive, Not Confrontational:</u> Use assertive communication techniques to convey your perspective and concerns while remaining respectful. Use "I statements" to express your thoughts and feelings, and actively listen to the salesperson's responses.

4. <u>Redirect the Conversation:</u> If a salesperson becomes too pushy or aggressive, redirect the conversation to focus on the facts, benefits, or any other relevant aspects of the product or service. Steer the conversation back to a more productive and balanced discussion.

Resolving Conflicts Professionally

Conflicts may arise during sales interactions but resolving them professionally is key to maintaining positive relationships. Consider these strategies for conflict resolution.

1. <u>Active Listening:</u> Listen attentively to the salesperson's perspective and demonstrate empathy.

Understand their concerns and motivations to find common ground for resolution.

2. Find Mutually Acceptable Solutions: Collaboratively explore potential solutions that address both party's needs and concerns. Look for compromises or alternative options that satisfy both sides.

3. Maintain Professionalism: Throughout the conflict resolution process, it's crucial to maintain professionalism. Avoid personal attacks, maintain a respectful tone, and focus on the issue at hand rather than getting caught up in emotions.

4. Be Prepared to Negotiate: Assertive communication involves finding middle ground and being open to negotiation. Clearly express your priorities and be willing to explore options that satisfy both parties.

By identifying challenging personality types, handling aggressive and pushy salespeople with assertiveness, resolving conflicts professionally, and employing assertive communication strategies, you can navigate difficult sales interactions more effectively and maintain your professionalism throughout the process.

Chapter 11: Cancelation and Reading Contracts

This is a chapter designed as a safeguard, in the event that, after reading everything prior to your sales meeting, you still feel like you are ready to make an immediate commitment. This is one of the most important chapters in this book. This book is not designed to keep you from making purchases or avoiding salespeople. It is designed to make sure you are not taken advantage of. It is almost impossible to avoid salespeople in today's world, especially if you own a home, and contracts are a part of life.

Cancellation

Every product or service you could possibly purchase has some kind of cancellation or return policy. Be aware that companies are not always required to disclose their cancellation or return policies to you at the time of sale. Even if they are, they are not always disclosed by the sales representative (this comes down to their own personal ethics). If they do not willingly disclose the policy, be sure to ask. These policies are governed by state and federal law. Make sure you read the policy if you are ever intending to make a commitment. Some of these are state specific so look them up if you have any concerns. If you change your mind about a purchase, do not allow a company or a sales representative to strong-arm you into keeping a product or service you no longer wish to keep. You have rights as a consumer, educate yourself and understand them.

Using Cancellation to Your Advantage

If you ever find yourself in a situation where you really want a product and are 100% convinced that this is your only chance to get this deal, carefully review the cancellation policy. If possible, you may be able to buy yourself time to do more research on the product and company. Adhere to the policy and promptly do your research so you can make an informed decision quickly within the time limits of the cancellation policy. If there is a loan involved, keep in mind, by doing this you risk taking multiple hits to your credit. Make sure to ask how many lenders will receive your information, but understand that once a company has your permission, they can send it to as many lenders as they wish. You have to decide for yourself what risks you are willing to take. I am not advocating for this approach. I am advocating that you negotiate the best deal possible for yourself first, before committing to a sale. Casual cancellation is not usually beneficial to you or the salesperson with whom you negotiated the deal.

Read Your Contract

I have said this more than once in this book: read your contract! This is a binding agreement. Be sure that you fully understand your financial or any other commitment before signing any contract or agreement.

Warranties

Do not forget to ask about the warranty! Almost every product comes with some kind of warranty. It is acceptable for you to ask for a copy of the warranty so you can read it before making any commitments. Warranties are often part of the sales pitch, but not always as good as they are initially presented to be. They will almost always have stipulations and rarely cover the entire product. Many are contingent on you performing routine maintenance or by you not adhering to a certain clause. It is easy for a company to void the warranty when it is not clearly understood by the buyer. Get very specific with your questions about maintenance and other expectations the company has for you. If the sales representative does not know the answers to your warranty questions, ask them to find out. They should be able to make a call for clarification. It's also very important to understand who backs these warranties and who will take care of you if something goes wrong. What good is a lifetime warranty if the company goes out of business? Warranties can be worth their weight in gold or not worth the paper they are written on. Make sure you understand them in detail.

By understanding your cancelation policy, thoroughly reading your sales contract and warranty, you can have peace of mind making purchasing commitments.

Chapter 12: Assessing Your Own Sales Skills

Assessing your own sales skills is crucial for personal growth and buying skills. In this chapter, we will discuss the importance of reflecting on your sales abilities, continuous improvement and learning, seeking feedback and mentorship, and becoming a savvy buyer. Keep in mind, while reading this chapter, that sales skills can be applied to many aspects of your day-to-day life. However, it is not necessary to have all these skills fully developed before you are able to hold your own with a sales representative.

Reflecting on Your Own Sales Abilities

Take the time to reflect on your sales abilities and identify areas for improvement. Consider the following points:

1. Strengths: Identify your strengths as a salesperson. What are you naturally good at? What skills or qualities set you apart? Are you good at communicating? Are you good at negotiating? Are you personable and easy to relate to? Are you a good listener?

2. Weaknesses: Recognize your weaknesses and areas that need improvement. What aspects of sales do you struggle with? What skills or knowledge gaps do you need to address?

3. Self-Awareness: Develop self-awareness by examining your behaviors, attitudes, and habits in sales interactions. How do you come across to others? Are there any patterns or tendencies you should be aware of?

4. Goal Alignment: Evaluate whether your sales interaction goals align with your personal values and

aspirations. Are you pursuing the right opportunities? Do you feel fulfilled by your experiences?

Becoming a Savvy Buyer

Understanding the buyer's perspective can enhance your sales skills. Here's how you can become a savvy buyer.

1. <u>Analyze your own buying experiences:</u> Reflect on your own experiences as a buyer. What factors influenced your purchasing decisions? What strategies or tactics did salespeople use that resonated with you or put you off?

2. <u>Be an attentive customer:</u> Pay attention to the sales techniques, communication styles, and customer service practices employed by salespeople. Evaluate their effectiveness and consider how you can incorporate successful strategies into your own negotiations.

3. <u>Seek insights from your peers:</u> Engage in conversations with your friends and family to gain insights into their buying preferences, pain points, and satisfaction levels. Use this information to refine your buying strategies.

The next two sections of this chapter will only be important to you if you wish to continue your growth as an everyday salesperson. Learning sales techniques can benefit you in your everyday life. Sales in its base form is ultimately just learning how to listen, understand, and communicate effectively with other individuals; it should not be about finding the high ground or taking advantage of people. Feel free to move on to the conclusion if you are uninterested in applying sales skills to your everyday life.

Continuous Improvement and Learning

Sales is a dynamic field, and continuous improvement is essential for success. Here's how you can continuously improve your sales negotiation skills.

1. Stay Updated: Keep yourself informed about industry trends, market changes, and new sales techniques. Read books, articles, and blogs related to sales and attend relevant webinars or workshops.

2. Attend Training and Development Programs or Seminars: Participate in sales training programs or workshops to enhance your knowledge and skills. Look for opportunities to learn from experienced sales professionals and industry experts.

3. Practice Role-Playing: Engage in role-playing exercises to simulate sales scenarios and practice different sales techniques. This allows you to refine your skills and gain confidence in various situations.

4. Set Learning Goals: Establish specific learning goals for yourself, such as improving your negotiation skills or enhancing your product knowledge. Break these goals down into actionable steps and track your progress.

5. Seek Feedback and Mentorship: Feedback and mentorship are invaluable resources for personal and professional growth. Request feedback, be open to constructive criticism, and use it as an opportunity to learn and improve.

6. Find a Mentor: Look for experienced sales professionals who can serve as mentors. They can provide guidance, share their knowledge and insights, and help you navigate challenges.

5. Network with Peers: Build relationships with other sales professionals to exchange ideas, seek advice, and learn from their experiences. Participate in industry

events, join professional associations, or engage in online communities.

By assessing your own sales skills, embracing continuous improvement and learning, seeking feedback and mentorship, and becoming a savvy buyer, you can enhance your sales abilities.

Chapter 13:

Becoming a Master of Negotiating with Salespeople

Congratulations! You have journeyed through this book and gained valuable insights into negotiating with salespeople. In this concluding chapter, let's recap the key strategies, emphasize the importance of embracing a collaborative approach, and highlight the confidence you have gained in navigating sales interactions.

Recap of Key Strategies

1. Understanding the World of Salespeople: Gain insights into the motivations, sales cycle, and psychological tactics used by salespeople to better navigate interactions.

2. Effective Communication Strategies: Master active listening, asking the right questions, managing objections, and maintaining assertiveness while building rapport.

3. Recognizing and Avoiding Manipulative Techniques: Develop awareness of high-pressure tactics, deceptive sales practices, and set boundaries to protect yourself from manipulation.

4. Negotiating Win-Win Solutions: Apply effective negotiation principles, identify common ground, and create mutually beneficial outcomes.

5. Ethical Considerations: Prioritize transparency, honesty, and ethical decision-making in sales interactions, setting ethical standards for yourself.

6. Dealing with Difficult Salespeople: Identify challenging personality types, handle aggressive

salespeople, resolve conflicts professionally, and employ assertive communication strategies.

7. Assessing Your Own Sales Skills: Reflect on your abilities, embrace continuous improvement and learning, seek feedback and mentorship, and become a savvy buyer.

Embracing a Collaborative Approach

In dealing with salespeople, it is essential to adopt a collaborative approach. Recognize that successful sales interactions are built on mutual understanding, respect, and shared goals. By fostering collaboration, you create an environment that encourages open communication, trust, and long-term partnerships. Remember that both parties have something to gain from a positive and productive relationship.

Confidence in Navigating Sales Interactions

By taking a journey through this book, you have gained knowledge, strategies, and skills that empower you to navigate sales interactions with confidence. You now possess the tools to set clear objectives, conduct thorough research, anticipate sales techniques, assert your needs, ask important questions, and negotiate win-win solutions. Trust in your abilities and believe in your capacity to achieve positive outcomes in sales interactions. In today's world, encounters with salespeople are unavoidable. With these newfound skills, you will not miss out on beneficial opportunities due to previous concerns about avoiding salespeople and the sales process.

By applying the strategies and approaches discussed in this book, you will become a master of dealing with salespeople. Your understanding of the sales process, effective communication techniques, ethical considerations, and collaborative mindset sets you apart as a skilled and confident buyer.

Remember, mastery is an ongoing process. Continue to seek opportunities for growth, refine your skills, and stay informed about emerging trends and best practices in sales. The world of sales is fast-paced and ever-evolving. Continue to invest in your personal and professional development to enhance your sales skills and stay ahead in the ever-evolving world of sales. By remaining adaptable and open to learning, you will continue to excel in your interactions with salespeople and many other aspects of your life.

Thank you for joining me on this journey. May your interactions with salespeople be fruitful, mutually beneficial, and ultimately satisfying. I wish you great success in your future endeavors!

Chapter 14: Comprehensive Checklist

Before Interactions:
- Set clear objectives for your interactions with salespeople.
- Conduct research on the salesperson and their company to gather information.
- Analyze your needs and requirements to understand what you are looking for.
- Anticipate common sales techniques to be better prepared.

During Interactions:
- Practice active listening to understand the salesperson's message and perspective.
- Ask the right questions to gather relevant information.
- Manage objections and negotiation by addressing concerns and seeking win-win solutions.
- Assertiveness and maintaining control over the conversation while being respectful.

Understanding Sales Tactics:
- Recognize upselling and cross-selling techniques used by salespeople.
- Be aware of tactics used to create a sense of urgency.
- Develop strategies to handle objections and overcome resistance.
- Prepare for discounts and pricing negotiations to ensure fair deals.

Building Strong Relationships:
- Prioritize trust and credibility in your interactions with salespeople.
- Foster long-term partnerships by delivering on commitments and providing value.

- Establish effective communication channels to facilitate ongoing collaboration.
- Balance assertiveness and cooperation to maintain a positive relationship.

Recognizing and Avoiding Manipulative Techniques:

- Stay vigilant to recognize high-pressure tactics employed by salespeople.
- Be aware of deceptive sales practices and protect yourself from being misled.
- Trust your instincts when something feels unethical or dishonest.
- Set clear boundaries and assert your needs to avoid manipulation.

Negotiating Win-Win Solutions:

- Apply principles of effective negotiation, such as preparing, listening, and offering options.
- Identify common ground to find mutually beneficial outcomes.
- Seek win-win solutions that address both your needs and the salesperson's goals.
- Recognize when it's necessary to walk away from a negotiation.

Ethical Considerations:

- Prioritize transparency and honesty in your sales interactions.
- Make ethical decisions by considering the impact on all parties involved.
- Recognize and avoid engaging in unethical practices.
- Set ethical standards for yourself and adhere to them in all your interactions.

Dealing with Difficult Salespeople:

- Identify challenging personality types and adjust your approach accordingly.

- Handle aggressive and pushy salespeople by maintaining your composure.
- Resolve conflicts professionally by focusing on problem-solving and open communication
- Use assertive communication strategies to express your needs and boundaries.
- Reflect on your own sales abilities and identify strengths and weaknesses.
- Commit to continuous improvement and learning by staying updated on industry trends.
- Seek feedback from colleagues, mentors, and customers to gain insights for growth.
- Embrace a mindset of constant learning and seek mentorship for guidance.

Cancellation and Reading Your Contract:
- Make sure to ask about and understand the cancelation policy.
- Read the contract and understand your commitment.
- Be thorough with your warranty.

Final Steps:
- Think of questions you would like to ask that have not been included in this book.
- Remember you have the money; you have the power.

By following this comprehensive checklist, you can effectively navigate interactions with salespeople, build strong relationships, and achieve successful outcomes. Remember, mastery in negotiating with salespeople is an ongoing process, so continuously revisit and refine your approach as you gain experience and encounter new situations.